How taking a risk can transform your community.

DANGEROUSLY

DR. LORI SALIERNO

FOREWORD BY COACH MARK RICHT

CELEBRATE LIFE INTERNATIONAL, INC.

Hope Dangerously: How Taking a Risk Can Transform Your Community
ISBN: 978-0-9826157-1-3

Published by
Celebrate Life International, Inc.

For information and inquiries, please contact Celebrate Life International, 3104 Creekside Village Dr, Suite 303, Kennesaw, GA 30144, or call (770) 529-7700, ext. 31, or e-mail *cli@CelebrateLife.org*.

Developmental Editing—Ben Stroup Enterprises, LLC (*www.benstroup.com*)—Greenbrier, TN

Strategy, Design, and Production—Root Radius, LLC (*www.rootradius.com*)—Acworth, GA

I dedicate this book to my late father, Gerald Marvel, who taught me to dream big and believe that with God, all things are possible, and take risks to attempt those things.

AUTHOR'S NOTE

A person who "hopes dangerously" is well acquainted with self-evaluation and constant improvement. That is why I decided to provide you with action items at the end of each chapter. As you reflect on the question and write down how you will put it into action, it is my hope that you will become a dangerous fighter against evil.

Together, we can challenge the cycle!

CONTENTS

FOREWORD

I dare say that all of us face challenges on a regular basis whether we accept them or not. And some of us even face more than our fair share of insurmountable challenges. I chose a career that seems to be filled with challenges of all sizes on a regular basis. When I take the time to look back and reflect on my career as a college football coach, I can see the long list of them. Some of those challenges seemed impossible to overcome at the time. My first season as Head Coach for the Georgia Bulldogs back in 2001 was up-and-down for me as well as the team. Each defeat taught me something and each victory validated that I had learned a particular lesson.

The lessons we choose to learn while we struggle through difficulties are some of the best education we can ever get. And that is something I appreciate about Lori Salierno. I first heard of Lori several years ago when a common friend shared with me about her work with at-risk kids. One thing led to another and my wife Katharyn and I ended up meeting Lori for lunch in Athens, GA. At that lunch I listened to her passion to help at-risk kids overcome insurmountable challenges and coach them through it so they can learn important life lessons. She spoke of kids in the public schools as well as kids assigned to her program by juvenile court judges. I heard about kids overcoming tough challenges thanks to volunteer mentors who willingly give of their time and effort to help them.

I get energized anytime I hear about people who give of themselves to help the next generation. Our football program at UGA is about helping young men succeed on and off the field. Yes, I want to win football games but I also want to see those young men win in life. The way we deal with the challenges we face as a team teaches our players invaluable lessons about how to overcome their own challenges in life and succeed.

In Hope Dangerously, Lori shares with us how the possibility of failure can also become an opportunity to succeed. Lori also shares stories from her Challenge the Cycle Tour which will surely encourage you in your own journey. In this book, she highlights something that few of us may willingly do in our daily lives. She purposely created her own seemingly insurmountable challenge. She did it in order to bring about good for the kids to whom she has dedicated her life. Her 46-day bicycle tour across the United States served as a call to action for thousands of people in our country. As she cycled, she called on every person she met to do something and help the millions of at-risk kids across our nation. She put some skin in the game and she is calling on all of us to do the same.

Whether we coach a football team, teach a Sunday school class in our church, or mentor an at-risk kid in our juvenile court systems, we can all do something for our next generation. Some kids may face more than their fair share of insurmountable challenges but each and every one of us can make a difference by helping them find victory in the lessons they learn.

Mark Richt
Head Coach,
University of Georgia Bulldogs Football Team
Athens, Georgia
Fall 2012
100th career victory (11th season at Georgia – 2011)
UGA Bulldogs – Southeastern Conference's Eastern Division Title – 2012

CHALLENGE THE CYCLE

There are 74 million people under the age of 18 in America today. We tend to think young people have a world of opportunity and hope ahead of them. But that's not true for all of them. Thirty percent will not finish high school, stunting their education and stifling their future job potential. And minorities in the group have only a 50 percent high school graduation rate. These young people are considered at-risk because they are likely to make decisions or choose activities that could harm them, get them into trouble, or—worse—cost them their lives.

The tragedy is at-risk kids are victims of a vicious downward cycle that results in generation after generation limited by the same prevailing realities: family troubles, limited education, broken homes, and an absence of someone who will love and invest in them. The good news is I believe there is hope for these kids, their families, and the communities in which they live. But it means doing things differently and challenging what many consider normal.

To demonstrate my commitment to reaching at-risk kids, I decided—at the age of 52—to ride a bicycle across America. With no previous cycling experience, I set out to do something that seemed impossible to me. Why would I challenge myself to do something like this? Because I believe all life is worth celebrating. Every child who is at-risk today doesn't have to remain a victim for life. What difference would biking across the country make for at-risk kids? It would give me a chance to raise awareness and support for my organization, Celebrate Life International, to help reverse the downward cycle so many kids face. It would also give me the chance to meet others located across the country with a similar passion for helping at-risk children.

Celebrate Life International is committed to changing the downward cycle many kids experience into an upward cycle through intervention, compassion, and re-education. These three things make up our *Teach One to Lead One*® Program that is transforming at-risk kids into responsible citizens with a better and brighter future.

The Challenge the Cycle tour took me across 15 states, totaling 3,284 miles, for the purpose of reaching and resourcing 10,000 at-risk kids for success. That seemed impossible at first, but I was determined to do whatever I had to do to make it a reality.

To prepare for this journey, I had to commit to a strict diet and intense daily training. I had to organize a team and secure funding. I had to map a course and plan for food, shelter, and the unexpected. I did all of this because I believe these kids are worth it. If I can ride across America, then together, we can change the future of a group of kids who desperately need someone to be on their side, help them change the cadence of their cycle, and give them a fighting chance for a better life for themselves and their children.

I want to share with you not only what I saw, experienced, and learned but how a whole generation can change . It was not an easy journey. There were plenty of scary moments along the way. But one thing is for sure: I was committed to let nothing get in the way of finishing what I had started. Too many people have already given up on these kids—even their families, in some cases. I was determined to finish because I didn't want to be just another person who gave up because the task at hand seemed impossible.

Do you believe every child—no matter who they are or where they come from—should have a chance at a better life? I do. And that's what this tour was all about. Together, we can challenge the cycle and inspire hope for at-risk kids and communities across the nation and around the worldthe task at hand seemed impossible.

Do you believe every child—no matter who they are or where they come from—should have a chance at a better life? I do. And that's what this tour was all about. Together, we can challenge the cycle and inspire hope for at-risk kids and communities across the nation and around the world.

"The good news is I believe there is hope for these kids, their families, and the communities in which they live."

Question: *Do you know of a young person or two in your circle of influence who could benefit from you lending them a hand?*

Action: *Schedule an appointment in your daily agenda for at least one act of kindness towards another human being. Who you are is more important than what you do because what you do comes from who you are.*

CHAPTER ONE

AN IMPOSSIBLE REALITY

"It always seems impossible until it's done."
—Nelson Mandela

We discover the impossible when we push ourselves beyond what we ever thought was possible. Challenge the Cycle was—by far—the most audacious thing I had ever done up to that point in my life. That's not to say I hadn't tried or accomplished big things in life. I have. But this challenge, in particular, took me way beyond what was comfortable and where I was thrust into the middle of the unexpected.

I remember one particular moment that shook me to my core. It was early in the morning, around 8:15 a.m. I was riding just outside downtown St. Louis, Missouri. The traffic was starting to pick up along my route. There were lots of on and off ramps with many vehicles entering and exiting the roadway. I was aware that the level of danger was high.

All of a sudden, I heard a BOOM! And I knew I had been hit by a car. I looked up at the compact car that was passing by, and my eyes locked with the female driver as she stared into her rearview mirror. She must have heard the same noise and was obviously curious about what had taken place. It took a few seconds before I felt the pain. I did not crash. My bike was not damaged. But her side-view mirror had come into contact with my hand, which was now throbbing.

I remember crying. I wasn't sure if I cried because of the throbbing pain in my hand or if I was just upset that the driver never bothered to stop and make sure I was OK. Nevertheless, it shook me up.

This was—by far—the scariest moment of the trip. Thankfully, the Tour Support Vehicle (TSV) that followed close by throughout the entire trip was there to help. I had to stop to deal with my injury and to complete a police report. The police officer actually urged me to get into the TSV in lieu of riding through downtown St. Louis.

In the end, I chose not to take the police officer's advice. If I got off my bike every time the road became difficult or dangerous, I would be spending a lot of time in the van instead of doing the bike tour. I was not going to give in to intimidation.

I decided to go back to the scene of the accident and start riding again. I couldn't give up on what I had set out to do. It meant too much to too many people. All I could think about was the need to continue to fight to bring awareness to the needs of at-risk kids. That was worth risking my own life.

Reaching at-risk youth and helping them change course isn't easy. It often seems hopeless, overwhelming, and impossible. But this is exactly how at-risk youth feel. They know firsthand how very grueling it is to overcome or break free from a difficult past.

At-risk kids are likely to have just one parent, some live in poverty and in tough neighborhoods. Others live in wealthy suburbs and are equally at-risk of dropping out of school, abusing drugs, and getting involved in delinquent behaviors. Their grades are not likely to be good, which will limit their potential or opportunity to go to college. Many at-risk youth are minorities. They are known for high rates of teen pregnancy, drug abuse, and alcohol abuse.

Many kids who fall into the at-risk category will have shorter life spans, lower IQs, and struggle with mental health problems. Many of these issues could be addressed through traditional medicine but aren't simply because of limited access to and affordability of health care or parents just don't seem to care enough to help them.

If you think reading about at-risk youth is difficult, try being one. Many just choose to give up and give in to what is around them, never realizing that they have the ability to break the cycle in their lives. That's why I couldn't quit when the road became difficult. That's why I couldn't stop. That's why I had to go back to the scene of the accident and start riding again. Fear was not going to stop me from fighting for a segment of our population many have already given up on.

Helping at-risk kids overcome the downward cycle can seem like an impossible reality. But that isn't necessarily true. It just takes a determination to see things differently and work until it is done.

"We discover the impossible when we push ourselves beyond what we ever thought was possible."

Question: *Is there something you are currently doing that you consider worthwhile but you want to quit doing because it's difficult?*

Action: *Identify as many timewasters as possible within your daily routine and decide to quit wasting that time. It is easier to put energy into worthwhile efforts when we are not exhausted by the meaningless things of life.*

CHAPTER TWO

A DANGEROUS PROPOSITION

"The world is a dangerous place. Not because of the people who are evil; but because of the people who don't do anything about it."
—Albert Einstein

When we face a reality that seems impossible, it always is followed by a dangerous proposition. Will we get involved and do something about it, or will we simply look in our rearview mirror as we leave the obstacle behind? The choice that we make says a lot about our values and what we really hold true. When reality intersects our lives and we are confronted with something that seems impossible and dangerous, we must decide what we will do next.

I was asked numerous times why I would attempt something like Challenge the Cycle, considering the danger and effort it would take. I gave the same answer every time: At-risk youth don't face danger some of the time. Rather, they face danger much of the time. That's why I am putting myself in a dangerous and seemingly impossible situation. It's for the kids who don't have a platform to speak about their realities and their needs. It's for the kids who don't have the privilege of growing up in a safe neighborhood and a nurturing family. They are the reason I accepted the dangerous proposition of cycling across the country to raise awareness and money. I wanted to give these kids a platform and bring attention to the danger they faced nearly every day of their lives.

One kid in particular comes to mind. His name is Ricardo. He came home one day to find his mother being stabbed by his stepfather. Ricardo used a bat to get this man away from his mom. He single-handedly saved her life. The police came and took his stepdad to jail and his mom to ICU.

When the principal of Ricardo's school heard what had happened, she connected him with one of our *Teach One to Lead One*® Programs where he could be nurtured by caring adults. Today, Ricardo is an honors student and is heading to college because adult volunteers agreed to mentor him. Because someone was willing to invest in Ricardo, he has a chance at a better life and the strength to break the cycle.

Another child who comes to mind was a little girl I met in Pocatello, Idaho. While in that town, I took a tour of a group home, met some important people who are part of the judicial process, and visited a place where kids who had been sexually abused come to heal. That's where I met Maria.

She was about 4 years old, had very dark hair, and big brown eyes. Maria's dad was with her and was obviously broken over the way his daughter was violated in such a personal way. I told Maria that I was cycling across the country for her. She didn't believe me at first. Honestly, I think she didn't believe that anyone would do that for her.

I told her that my cycling across the country was bringing attention to little boys and girls like her who needed to know that lots of people cared deeply for kids like her and wanted to help them. She didn't know what to think.

I gave her a water bottle and told her that every time she drank from this water bottle she would know that there were countless people fighting to help little girls like her heal inside and have a much happier future.

Maria allowed me to give her a hug before I left. As I turned to go, I caught sight of the sadness in her dad's eyes. I get choked up when I think about the frightening life Maria has faced so far.

Kids like Ricardo and Maria deserve to have hope. I may be attempting dangerous things along my journey, but every night I get a warm shower, a hot meal, and safe place to sleep. That's not true for everyone, especially children in dangerous situations like the ones Ricardo and Maria have faced.

Reaching out to help at-risk kids is a dangerous proposition. We have to get involved, open our hearts, and care about their futures. But if we don't embrace this dangerous proposition, we pass them by with only a glance in our rearview mirrors as we go on about our lives, relatively unaffected by their pain.

"When we face a reality that seems impossible, it always is followed by a dangerous proposition."

Question: *What is your response when faced with a dangerous situation that will ultimately be of great help to others?*

Action: *Find a need in your community that will require a response that appears dangerous to you and find someone to help you get it done. When we do not respond to opportunities in our path, we are, in reality, deciding that we don't care about them.*

CHAPTER THREE

THE RELENTLESS CLIMB

*"If you're trying to achieve, there will be roadblocks.
I've had them; everybody has them. But obstacles don't
have to stop you. If you run into a wall, don't turn
around and give up. Figure out how to climb it, go
through it, or work around it."*
—Michael Jordan

Any time we attempt things that are seemingly impossible, we must expect that our endurance will be tested. The life experiences we cherish are the ones in which we overcome adversity. It is in the climb that we learn the most about who we are, what we really believe, and how we see the world around us.

My relentless climb began way before I rode the first mile of the Challenge the Cycle tour.

I knew the challenge itself would be tough, but I had no idea just how tough the training would be. The preparation for the journey pushed me beyond what I thought I could do. Training made for early days and late nights—and my life didn't go on pause. I still had to go to the office, get work done, and make sure Celebrate Life

International stayed on course.

There were times during my training when I did things I didn't even think were possible. (And I hurt in places I wasn't even aware existed.) Preparation was an important part of the uphill journey. It prepared me not only physically but also mentally to endure the cycling adventure I was about to embark upon.

Another part of the tour preparation was raising the $25,000 we needed to conduct the Challenge the Cycle tour. I personally didn't have that money, nor did our organization. I didn't know how we were going to pull it off, but I just knew it had to happen.

One day I decided to make a phone call to someone who had been a close friend to my dad. I couldn't get him off my mind. I wasn't sure what I was doing or what we would even talk about. Before we hung up, he asked if it would be all right if he sent me a check for $25,000. I didn't know what to say other than yes. The whole experience was beyond belief.

I immediately went back to the office and told our operations director about my phone conversation. He smiled and indicated it was time to get a bike and start getting ready because the Challenge the Cycle tour was now a sure thing.

This cycling endeavor taught me how important it was to prepare in advance of the journey and to depend on other people along the way. Yes, I was the one who had to put my feet on the pedals to turn the wheels of the bike. But at no point along the way was I ever really alone. I had a support team that was always nearby to help in any way they could.

And there were the people like my dad's friend who made the tour financially possible, along with the countless program leaders and mentors across the country who carry forward the *Teach One to*

Lead One® banner. Their courage to never give up is changing lives all across the country and around the world.

We are not the only ones who face a relentless climb. The at-risk kids we seek to help face a similar climb in their everyday lives. Sadly, many of them find it impossible because there is no one available to support and sustain them along the way.

Every child deserves to have at least one person who believes that a better life is possible and is confident that these kids can accomplish far more than they ever thought possible. Helping at-risk kids in their relentless climb is the least we can do when so many of us—including me—have been blessed far beyond our basic needs.

We should never let what we can't do keep us from what we can do. Today, we must push through even the toughest, most rigorous ascent. Only then will we reach the peak and see lives changed forever.

There are simply too many lives at stake to let a relentless climb keep us from taking the journey. We must figure out how to climb it, go through it, or work around it.

"There are simply too many lives at stake to let a relentless climb keep us from taking the journey."

Question: *What are you currently doing to prepare yourself for times of adversity?*

Action: *Identify those who can help you navigate through times of adversity. Adversity brings about the best learning opportunities that we will ever have.*

Sharing with *Teach One to Lead One*® students in Vancouver, WA, why young people are the reason for the Challenge the Cycle Tour

Taking every opportunity to share with news outlets about issues affecting youth in America

Exhausted after outrunning a ferocious-looking dog in Kentucky

Posing for a quick photo at the end of a hot 100-mile day in the middle of a hay field in Kansas

Hydrating frequently along the route was of paramount importance regardless of temperature and terrain

DRINKWATER PASS
ELEV. 4212

Speaking with Juvenile Court Judge, Bryan Murray, in Pocatello, ID, about challenges facing children in his community

Starting the day with a much-appreciated police escort through the streets of Jefferson City, MO

Riding into Portland, OR, in what turned out to be the only day of rain on the tour (out of 46 days of riding)

Celebrating at the summit of Cameron Pass in the Colorado Rockies—highest point of the tour

Enjoying a quick snack provided by the volunteer support team who waited at designated places along the route

Meeting early in the morning with a group of cyclists in Emerson, GA, who joined as an escort for the last 10 miles of the tour

Learning from local law enforcement about youth programs and community efforts that can make a positive difference in a community

Icing a swollen hand that was hit by a passing car whose driver did not bother to stop

Cycling mile after mile through rural Georgia to complete the 3,248-mile Challenge the Cycle Tour

Listening to a warm "Welcome Home" from Mayor Tommy Allegood at North Cobb High School in Acworth, GA

There's No Place Like Home!

Crossing the Mississippi River and turning southeast towards home in Atlanta, GA

CHAPTER FOUR

THE POSSIBILTY OF FAILURE

"Never, never, in nothing great or small, large or petty, never give in except to convictions of honour and good sense. Never yield to force; never yield to the apparently overwhelming might of the enemy."
—*Winston Churchill*

Every great victory in life comes with the possibility of utter failure. No matter how many times I've overcome the obstacles in front of me, the fear of failure grips me as I move forward into a danger zone. The most important task in those moments is to keep moving forward—even when you feel like giving up.

I remember standing at the base of the Rocky Mountains at Cache National Forest in northern Utah. The mountains seemed so tall. The largeness of the landscape around me seemed to swallow me whole. I couldn't fight back the tears, so I just let them fall. I didn't know what else to do. I knew failure was a great possibility based on what I could see in front of me.

In that moment, the possibility of failure felt so real. I didn't think it would be possible to do what I had intended to do. You know those times when your mind starts racing about identifying anything and everything that could go wrong? That's what I was experiencing in that moment, and it almost paralyzed me.

I was scared by the magnitude of the task ahead. It was a tough road—but not as tough as everyday life can be for the at-risk kids I was riding for. They face some impossible obstacles, yet many of them press on with unwavering optimism that tomorrow is another day. If they can live life with that kind of strength, I knew I could approach these mountains in the same way.

I pedaled just like I had from the beginning. A downward cycle and an upward cycle...again and again and again. Soon I was moving ahead, and as I climbed the mountain, I could feel the change in altitude. The air became a little thinner and my breathing changed slightly, but I never stopped moving forward.

When I reached the summit of 10,296 feet at Cameron Pass in Colorado, it was an awesome experience. My support team and I paused to celebrate for about an hour. The view was incredible, and I don't remember a Snickers bar tasting so good! It satisfied my craving for food and helped make the moment even sweeter.

That wouldn't be the last time during the tour that I would come face to face with the possibility of failure. Someone had spoken with me about his experience on a tour like the one I was on and had warned me about "hitting the wall."

If you've ever been a part of an endurance sport like running, swimming, or cycling, you know exactly what I'm talking about. If you haven't, there is a good chance you know someone who has talked about this phenomenon.

The "wall" is not real; it's a metaphor. It's an experience that is hard to describe. It stops you emotionally as if you had hit a physical wall.

I certainly hit mine during the tour. It came after a good cycling day where I had covered more than 100 miles. We were settled for the night and ready to head out to dinner when I started crying. No matter what I tried, I couldn't stop the tears.

I called one of my team members and explained why I wouldn't be able to go to dinner. The team decided to adjust the plan, ordering take-out food instead and bringing it back to my hotel room. That was a special night when the encouragement of my team helped me push through the wall that was holding me back.

When you work with at-risk kids, you know that the possibility of failure is high. There is so much out of your control. Nevertheless, we can never, never, never give up—even when we don't feel like moving forward. I was determined not to give up on myself or on these kids during the tour, even when I had hit the wall. I was going to endure until the end, one pedal at a time.

> *"Every great victory in life comes with the possibility of utter failure."*

Question: *What do you do when gripped by fear of the unknown or the possibility of failure?*

Action: *Face the fear of the unknown by focusing on the ultimate benefit of your efforts. A very large mission or project can be accomplished by small and consistent steps.*

CHAPTER FIVE

THE OPPORTUNITY TO SUCCEED

*"Success is to be measured not so much by the position
that one has reached in life as by
the obstacles which he has overcome."*
—Booker T. Washington

With the possibility of failure comes the opportunity to succeed. That's what we have to keep reminding ourselves when we "hit the wall" along the way. It doesn't just happen once; it happens over and over again. We must choose every time if we will continue, turn back, or give up completely.

I estimate that I pedaled approximately 847,000 times over the course of the Challenge the Cycle tour. I didn't think about this number while I was on the tour. Instead, I set out just to accomplish each day's goal. The team would tell me, "Lori, today is a 100-mile day." Or, "You go girl—just 8 miles to go!" Or, "Can you handle another 5 miles?" If I did that consistently, I would reach my ultimate goal and experience success. I had the opportunity to succeed with each turn of my bike's pedals.

As I was riding on the Katy Trail in Missouri, I saw three elementary age boys resting along the side. I rode passed them and waved. The boys seemed to me the picture of childhood summer: They were on their bikes, shirts off, laughing, and having a carefree time.

I continued to ride until I caught up with the volunteers who had gone ahead of me. There I stopped to have my morning break and snacks. Eventually, those same boys caught up with me.

They were very talkative and began to share about their lives in the small town that we were in. One boy said, "I am the smart one of the three." A second boy said, "And I am the most athletic one of the three." The third boy said, "And I am the 'nothing' one of the three."

I shared with this third boy that there was no such thing as a "nothing" person. We all have strengths and talents; we just have to discover them. As I talked with these three boys, I realized that the whole bike ride was for boys like these: to reach one child at a time.

Even though I was riding on behalf of 20 million at-risk kids in our country, it is so important to look at and see each child individually. We have a lot of kids who think they are "nothing" kids. Challenge the Cycle is an effective way to share hope and let kids know that they are "something" kids.

If we will reach one student at a time and do that over and over and over again, we will experience the compound effect of reaching a whole generation. That is what the opportunity for success looks like. It's not just doing it once with one child. We build momentum over time through consistency of effort and staying the course. In time, with each push and each effort, we will see our work multiplied through the lives of the at-risk kids we reach.

Each at-risk child affords us the opportunity to challenge the cycle. That's how we'll change an entire generation and rewrite the life story of more than 20 million at-risk kids in our country. It will happen one child at a time. In time, we'll experience a compounding effect that will ignite a level of momentum opening opportunities for success in the lives of children who need it most.

"We all have strengths and talents; we just have to discover them."

Question: *Have you created an inventory of your strengths and talents? If so, are you maximizing them?*

Action: *Write in a journal your life experiences from the past where you used your talents and strengths—and succeeded. Past successes provide us with firm confidence to take on greater opportunities in the future.*

CHAPTER SIX

A VOICE FOR HOPE

"Love recognizes no barriers. It jumps hurdles, leaps fences, and penetrates walls to arrive at itsdestination full of hope."
—Maya Angelou

Hope is one of the most powerful forces we can harness in our lives. It can propel us forward and can offer the strength we need in our moment of weakness. Without hope, there is no chance to challenge the cycle.

I remember needing some hope as I found myself riding into Jefferson City, Missouri. It had been a long day, and I was ready to call it a night. But when I arrived at the hotel, there were a few journalists there to take some pictures, film some video footage, and interview me about the Challenge the Cycle tour.

While I was finishing my interview, the hotel manager found me and asked if he could talk to me. I agreed even though I wasn't sure what I was getting myself into.

He explained there was a group of 100 kids who needed to hear my story. They happened to be at a leadership camp called "Cycle." This camp was for the top 100 leadership students in Missouri. He wanted me to address the students about what I was doing and why.

I couldn't believe the similarities between the tour and this event. I agreed to meet these young leaders.

As I spoke to the students, I reminded them they are impacting their own generation already. They might be at the camp to learn how to be better leaders, but they were clearly already leaders in their own right. I told them I was riding across the country for kids who would never be asked to participate in an event like the one they were at- kids who were just as important as these impressive youth.

I explained that there were other students in their schools, neighborhoods, and churches who were in trouble, in need of help, hope, and support. I challenged this group of young leaders to reach out to those in their own generation who were in need. Just as I was being a voice of hope to them, I was encouraging them to be the voice of hope in their own circles of influence.

As I rode out of Jefferson City the next morning, I was still reflecting on the whole experience. There were countless times along the way when unexpected opportunities like that would emerge. It taught me that when you prepare yourself and push through the obstacles, the needs would often find you.

Many times adults will be touched and moved by what we do through the *Teach One to Lead One*® Program. They will be motivated by the story behind the Challenge the Cycle tour. But they won't know if they can make a difference. I tell everyone interested in joining us in some specific way that when we put our passion into action, those who need what we have to offer will suddenly appear.

You'll talk to a kid who needed to hear your story. You'll find an opportunity to generously support a new *Teach One to Lead One*® Program in your community where you'll discover needs you never knew existed. Hope has a way of making itself known in the midst of the journey.

Those who participate as mentors in the *Teach One to Lead One*® Program know that their effort, sacrifice, and investment in at-risk kids are fundamental. It is through them that we continue to reach kids who desperately need to be reminded that they have something to be hopeful about.

There is something that happens when we are willing to "put some skin in the game" to reach at-risk kids. We become a voice for hope that speaks into the lives of a new generation of leaders. We aren't just helping these kids avoid the pitfalls in front of them today. That is only part of the story. The rest of the story is that we are preparing them to do the same for someone else in the future.

Hope multiplies when we love one another and demonstrate that love through our actions. The Challenge the Cycle tour was not merely an athletic endeavor. It was a demonstration of hope and love to kids who are worth fighting for, worth sacrificing for, and worth reaching.

At-risk kids need someone to speak hope into their lives. When we do, we unleash the power of love to transform them at their core and set them on a path to become world changers forever. The voice of hope is a powerful catalyst for change within communities and in an entire generation.

"The voice of hope is a powerful catalyst for change within communities and in an entire generation."

Question: *How are you putting "skin in the game" to challenge a negative cycle in your sphere of influence?*

Action: *Identify a need in your community that matters to you and make clear to others what must be done. Positive changes in history have always required clear communication of the need and of the action needed to meet the need.*

CHAPTER SEVEN

THE END IS JUST A NEW BEGINNING

*"The great use of life is to spend it for
something that will outlast it."*
—Charles Mayes

The date was August 4, 2012. The time had finally arrived. I was
ready to bring this cross-country ride to an end. I remember getting
up and feeling really excited about what had taken place along the
journey. I never felt alone because I knew that so many others were
helping support what I was doing through generous donations,
sharing information about Challenge the Cycle, and participating
in our work.

I always wondered what it would feel like to do something that I
never thought was possible. At my age, I never thought I would be
able to ride 3,284 miles across 15 states, but I did. And I did it for
the same kids I've been fighting for most of my adult life—at-risk
kids who need hope that tomorrow can be better than today.

I reflected on the journey that had brought me to this point. I
thought about the majesty of Mt. Hood in Oregon, about riding
over the Rocky Mountains, passing by the wildfires of Colorado,

withstanding the winds of Kansas, and enduring the heat of Missouri, and maneuvering shoulder-less county roads in Kentucky, Tennessee, and Alabama. Now it was time to ride home to Acworth, Georgia.

I felt an amazing sense of privilege. I loved being a voice for the voiceless by using my platform to shine a light on kids without a voice or a platform. Every day I suited up, got on my bike, and rode. Even when I didn't want to, I did it. I wasn't going to let those kids down.

I suited up that morning, got on my bike, and started riding toward North Cobb High School. Before I got there, a group of more than 20 riders joined me on the last day of riding, escorting me the final 10 miles to the school.

Together, we rode in complete solidarity. I may have been a lone cyclist on this journey, but I would finish it with many who were ready to help me carry forward the *Teach One to Lead One*® philosophy. It was surreal.

When we arrived, I let the group go ahead of me into the stadium. I patiently waited to hear my name called. Then I heard a voice say, "Ladies and Gentlemen, let's welcome Lori Salierno home." I rode into the stadium and onto the track. I made a victory lap while music played and people clapped and cheered. The mayor was there along with others from the area. I was overwhelmed by all the support. My spirit soared. I could hardly fight back the tears.

I had accomplished exactly what I had set out to accomplish. More importantly, the message had gone out across the country loud and clear:

• We can challenge the cycle.

- It looks impossible.

- But it can be accomplished.

The only two requirements are hope in the future of at-risk kids and freely giving of our time and resources. If we possess both of those things, then the work will be done, lives will be changed, and communities transformed.

This ride was not the end. Rather, it was just a new beginning.

"This ride was not the end. Rather, it was just a new beginning."

Question: *How often do you do your personal best in all aspects of your life?*

Action: *Identify those areas of your life where improvement is needed and set goals that will mark new beginnings. Projects that end with excellence bring energy to new beginnings.*

WHAT YOU DO MATTERS

People often tell me how much they connect with what we're doing through the *Teach One to Lead One*® Program. They confess how much they want to do something that matters too. However, they aren't sure how to get started.

Let me make this very clear: just do something. It's as simple as that. You don't have to be qualified to invest in someone else; you simply have to be available and willing to give of yourself to make a difference in someone else's life.

I did something crazy to help. I rode 3,284 miles across 15 states by myself. At 52, I'm way beyond the age group that is likely to consider taking on such a task.

It was hard—very hard. I had to train, follow a strict diet, and push through the days when I just wanted to give up. And, yes, there were countless things that could have—and did—go wrong along the way. (For example, I got lost for four hours in Colorado where there was no cell phone service!)

But something that is worth doing—actions that create change in life—requires risk. We have to be willing to lay ourselves out for the causes and people we believe in. That's what creating a legacy is all about.

One thing is certain: If you never take action, you will never make a difference. What you do matters more than what you say. If our actions don't match our words, then people will sense that we aren't committed to the things we're talking about. However, if our actions back up our words, people will notice and rally around to support and encourage the cause.

You have the capacity to inspire people to care about at-risk kids. The *Teach One to Lead One®* Program works because people like you believe in these kids as much as I do and are willing to give time and money to ensure they have a legitimate chance for a better life than the one they were born into.

Without volunteers, mentors, and investors (donors), we wouldn't exist. This work is more than my personal agenda or a political stump speech. It is a direct assault on culture and the negative forces that are keeping at-risk kids from realizing all the potential for good they have in their lives.

Together, we can challenge the cycle and:

• *Reclaim the lives of those who have been pushed aside.*

• *Create opportunities for those who have none.*

• *Inspire hope for those who have lost their way.*

• *Encourage individuals to take responsibility for their decisions and lives.*

• *Rebuild communities and homes that have been broken.*

You can be part of the solution. You can make a difference. Whatever it costs, wherever it leads, however it plays out, these kids deserve our very best.

What you do matters.

MENTORS

PROGRAMS

TOOLS

HOW YOU CAN GET INVOLVED

Celebrate Life International needs your help! If you're interested in challenging the destructive cycle that is limiting the potential of at-risk kids, their families, and society, then join us in this revolution of hope. There are three specific ways you can get involved:

DONATE.

Generous contributions from financial partners like you are essential to our ability to continue to support our program leaders and volunteers. Whether you want to make a one-time gift or a monthly gift, a large gift or a small gift, please know that your generosity will be maximized for impact. If you'd like, we'd be happy to put you in touch with a program director, so you can see what a difference having the Teach One to Lead One® Program can make—or is already making—in your community.

GET TRAINED AND BECOME A MENTOR.

The success of our efforts is dependent upon volunteers. The work is too vast for any paid staff—no matter how large—to accomplish. If there is already a program in your area, they are likely looking for volunteers. You can participate as a mentor for kids who have few—

if any—role models to look up to. This is a great way to get to know the people in your community and be a source of encouragement and strength for kids who are often left out, overlooked, and counted out.

START A *TEACH ONE TO LEAD ONE*® PROGRAM IN YOUR COMMUNITY.

No one person can accomplish this task alone. Together, we can do more than we ever thought possible. Consider starting a Teach One to Lead One® Program in your community. We'll be here to walk through the process with you every step of the way. Countless other volunteers—just like you—have done so. You can be part of the solution and help these at-risk kids find the strength to accomplish far more than they ever thought they could.

ABOUT CELEBRATE LIFE INTERNATIONAL

CELEBRATE LIFE INTERNATIONAL was established with the goal of positively impacting young people by bringing them to an understanding of absolute truth through healthy mentoring relationships. The organization's name was specifically selected to describe the approach that Dr. Lori Salierno wanted to use to help young people find their unique purpose in life. The organization is designed to lift up tomorrow's leaders for restoring the family and transforming society—Developing Leaders of Integrity.

In its first year, the organization reached thousands of students, women, and leaders through conferences challenging them to live beyond mediocrity and make a positive contribution to those around them. Celebrate Life International's first office was located in a spare bedroom in Dr. Salierno's home. It wasn't long before the organization rented space at a local church to make room for its first two employees. By 1999, the organization had outgrown the space at the church and relocated to a larger facility in Acworth, Georgia. During the same year, the Celebrate Life International staff completed a youth development curriculum and piloted its first program under the name *Teach One to Lead One*®. This program spawned a life philosophy touching on multiple areas of character and leadership development.

In 2002, the *Teach One to Lead One*® philosophy was adapted to the needs of the juvenile court system and a court specific program was piloted with a group of high school students on probation. The court program has since expanded to include middle school probationers. In 2004, Celebrate Life International took on a new venture working with at-risk kids through a summer day camp, and in 2007, the *Teach One to Lead One*® OnDemand camp was launched for children who aren't connected to a school or juvenile court class.

Celebrate Life International continued to grow. A new delivery model of the *Teach One to Lead One*® philosophy was created to expand the reach of the program. In 2008, Celebrate Life International launched *Teach One to Lead One*®–Living Principles!™, a volunteer-led mentoring program that streamlined many of the curriculum elements while maintaining the core concept of Universal Principles. By 2010, the *Teach One to Lead One*® curriculum was modified again, still utilizing an all-volunteer mentoring structure but updating many of the materials. Then in 2011, the program was adapted for elementary-age children with the first group of 4th graders completing the *Teach One to Lead One*® program in early 2012.

In the United States, the *Teach One to Lead One*® Program is currently delivered to youth in Alabama, California, Colorado, Florida, Georgia and Washington, and has been active in many other states as well. Internationally, Celebrate Life South Africa™ was established in 2007, and there is a strong *Teach One to Lead One*® program presence in Australia, Ecuador, and El Salvador. The program is currently available in English, Spanish and Russian.

Dr. Lori Salierno currently holds the position of President and CEO of Celebrate Life International. A national board of directors oversees the corporation and acts as a catalyst for the expansion of the *Teach One to Lead One®* philosophy and program in order to continue to have an even larger positive impact on at-risk kids in the future.

Learn more by visiting *www.celebratelife.org.*